Wrecked!

Mysteries and disasters at sea

Jan Bassett is an historian with a particular interest in Australian history. She has taught in schools and universities, but now is a full-time writer.

Jan has always been intrigued by stories of shipwrecks, and amazed by the endurance shown by the survivors. Two of her favourite places in the world are Cornwall, in England, and Phillip Island, both the scene of many shipwrecks.

Jan has written a number of books, including *Guns and Brooches* (1992), about Australia's army nurses, *The Concise Oxford Dictionary of Australian History* (1986, second edition 1994), and she has edited a collection of travel writing, called *Great Southern Landings* (1995).

Wrecked!

Mysteries and disasters at sea

Jan Bassett

A LITTLE ARK BOOK

ALLEN & UNWIN

© text, Jan Bassett, 1996
© b/w illustrations, John Nicholson, 1996

This book is copyright under the Berne Convention.
No reproduction without permission.
All rights reserved.

First published 1996
A Little Ark Book
Allen & Unwin Pty Ltd
9 Atchison Street
St Leonards, NSW 2065
Australia
Phone: (61 2) 9901 4088
Fax: (61 2) 9906 2218
E-mail: 100252.103@compuserve.com

10 9 8 7 6 5 4 3 2 1

National Library of Australia
Cataloguing-in-Publication entry:

Wrecked!: mysteries and disasters at sea.
Bibliography.
Includes index.
ISBN 1 86448 089 0.

1. Shipwrecks – Australia – Juvenile literature.
I. Bassett, Jan, 1953- .
II. Title. (Series: True stories (St.Leonards, N.S.W.)).
910.45

Cover illustration by Mark Sofilas
Text illustrations by John Nicholson
Designed by Mark Carter
Printed in Australia by McPherson's Printing Group, Maryborough, Victoria

Photo credits: Thanks to Catherine O'Rourke for picture research.
• Scene below deck, from the *Illustrated London News*, 1884, reproduced by permission of the State Library of Victoria • Photo of the *Speke* figurehead, courtesy of the Phillip Island Historical Centre • Photo of the *Batavia* wreck by Jeremy Green, © Western Australian Maritime Museum
• Stamp from the Australian Bicentennial, II: Terra Australis – Coastal Shipwrecks issue, courtesy of the National Philatelic Collection, Australia Post • Photo of Great Barrier Reef, © Gary Bell/Ocean Wide Images
• Photo of the *Bounty*, courtesy of Bounty Cruises, Sydney • Eliza Fraser, reproduced by permission of the State Library of New South Wales
• Eva Carmichael, Tom Pearce, Loch Ard Peacock, spike and latch, courtesy of the Flagstaff Hill Maritime Museum, Warrnambool
• Metropolitan Police reward poster, reproduced by permission of The Archives Authority of New South Wales • Sketch of the scene at Bermagui, based on the map from the *NSW Votes and Proceedings of the Legislative Assembly during the session of 1883, Vol II*

Contents

	Shipboard life	8
1	The Story of the *Speke*	11
2	Batavia's Graveyard	18
3	The Mutiny on the *Bounty*	26
4	The Adventures of Eliza Fraser	37
5	Australia's Worst Shipwreck	47
6	Eva's Story	59
7	'Grace Darling of the West'	69
8	The Bermagui Mystery	74
9	The Ancient Wreck	84
	Glossary	92
	Further reading	93
	Index	95

WRECKED!

Acknowledgments

I am very grateful to Olga Abrahams, Janette Bomford, Nicholas Bomford, Gary Boulter, Mark Carter, Andrew Demetriou, Clare Ellison, David Ellison, Sue Flockhart, Frank Lyons, Una Lyons, Cherry McFee, Alan Mason, John Nicholson, Nancy Osborne, Tim Osborne, David Preston, Sue Preston, Rosalind Price, Dr Carolyn Rasmussen, Maggie Richardson, Cathy Smith, Mark Sofilas and Louise Sweetland for their help with this book. Special thanks also to the staff and patrons of the Killarney Hotel.

PACIFIC OCEAN
Jakarta
INDIAN OCEAN
TIMOR
AUSTRALIA
Houtman Abrolhos
King Island
Bass Strait

WRECKED!

Shipboard life

Many years ago, my Nana used to tell me stories about Australia's past. The one that I most liked was about a ship that was wrecked in 1906. Since then, I have always been fascinated by shipwrecks and other stories of the sea.

Europeans visiting Australia and nearby islands from the 1600s onwards, maybe even earlier, faced many dangers. Their small wooden sailing ships had to battle across thousands of kilometres of ocean. In those days, long before the invention of satellites and computers, captains had to navigate by the sun and stars. Their charts often were not very accurate and there were few lighthouses to guide them along the coastlines.

Tempers sometimes flared in the overcrowded, cramped little ships. Men were forced to live in close quarters for months on end, while their womenfolk and families were back in the home countries. Supplies of fresh food soon ran out and the men had to eat dried meat and biscuits. Life on board the ships was hard and demanding, and it must have been an overwhelming relief for the sailors to arrive on warm, sunny islands where the people were friendly. Sometimes the sailors would run away, deserting the ship, and other times it seems as if they almost went mad with the freedom of these places, after

Scene below deck

WRECKED!

shipboard life. Discipline then was harsh, and punishments included torture. Mutiny was punishable by hanging.

Migrants coming from Europe to Australia during the 1800s faced many hardships and dangers. Poverty and a lack of opportunities forced some to leave their homes. Others left because they had a strong sense of adventure. All hoped for better lives in their new country, halfway across the world. Leaving was hard. As they stepped aboard ships at the beginning of their long voyages, most knew that they probably would never see their family in the old country again. Conditions were often uncomfortable, with little space or privacy for individuals or families. And there was an ever-present risk of shipwreck.

Ships often sank very fast after striking reefs, leaving victims trapped below deck. Sometimes there was no time to launch lifeboats, or they sank after being swamped with water or being smashed against rocks and wreckage. Few passengers or crew knew how to swim. Amid the horror, however, brave feats and remarkable rescues occurred. Once on land, some survivors also showed great courage and endurance.

Although we know a lot about shipwrecks from eyewitness accounts and the work of archaeologists and treasure-seekers, many questions remain unanswered. See whether you can unravel some of the mysteries in this book.

1 The story of the **Speke**

Nana's stories

When I was young, I used to spend my holidays at my mother's family's farm on Phillip Island. It was close to Ventnor beach and was called 'The Pines'. My bed was a couch in my grandparents' bedroom. As Nana unpinned her long hair in the flickering lamplight, she told me stories about her girlhood on the island, while outside the wind howled through the pine trees and around the old house.

Nana was born in 1891, and had lived at 'The Pines' since 1905. Her mother's parents had settled on the island in the 1860s. Edie, my Nana, was the eldest of five children. After her father died, she helped her mother run the farm. Like other islanders, they grew chicory – chicory root is dried to make a drink like coffee. If you visit Phillip Island today, you can still see chicory kilns in which local farmers used to dry their crops. Sometimes Nana's neighbour, Paddy Phelan, used to help at 'The Pines'. He lived in a thatched cottage near the beach where tourists now watch the fairy penguins come ashore. But

> ... there were wild seas and gale-force winds in Bass Strait
> ... sailors came to the door, half-drowned

11

WRECKED!
**The story of
the** Speke

in those days Phillip Island was a remote, isolated place, with only a few hundred settlers. There was no bridge from the mainland to the island – you could only get there by boat.

My favourite story was about a shipwreck that happened when Nana was a girl. The *Speke* was one of the biggest three-masted steel sailing ships ever built. It was headed for Geelong to collect a load of wheat to take to Britain. But there were wild seas and gale-force winds in Bass Strait, and the *Speke* was wrecked on the south-west coast of Phillip Island. Some of the bedraggled sailors struggled across the island to 'The Pines' for help. Edie was aged 14 when the sailors came to the door, half-drowned and on their last legs. The captain gave her a compass box and a button from his jacket.

On the rocks

Captain Tilston and the 26 crew on board the *Speke* had sailed from Sydney on 12 February 1906. After they reached the Victorian coast and the weather became stormy, the captain made a terrible mistake. Perhaps he mistook a bushfire burning on Phillip Island for the lights of a town or a navigation light. It was whispered that wreckers deliberately used false lights to lure the ship to disaster, but that probably isn't true... Whatever the reason, on 21 February the *Speke* came dangerously close to shore, in the area between Cape Woolamai and Pyramid Rock.

> ... **the** Speke **struck rocks 50 metres from the beach**

By next morning, the ship was not far from the Nobbies. The wind and waves tossed it around like a toy boat, even though it was about 95 metres long. The ship was hard to steer because it was sitting up high in the water, with only sandbags as ballast to weigh it down. Closer and closer it came to the rough black rocks near one end of Kitty Miller's Bay. The crew dropped two anchors overboard, but the chain on one broke and the other anchor dragged on the seabed. That afternoon the ship struck rocks 50 metres from the beach.

Four men managed to get into a lifeboat. But a big wave caught one of them, Frank

WRECKED!
The story of the Speke

> **'DEAD MEN TELL NO TALES'**
>
> There are many stories about wreckers who operated around the rugged coast of Cornwall, in south-west England. Some looted ships after they had been wrecked, but others are said to have **caused** wrecks by putting up lights in bad weather which innocent sailors confused with the beams from lighthouses. Even the keepers of the lighthouse on the Scilly Islands, in the 1700s, allegedly let the light burn low or even go out altogether during storms so that wrecks occurred. The worst wreckers are thought to have killed any survivors from the wrecks, because 'dead men tell no tales'. You can read about fictional Cornish wreckers in Daphne du Maurier's famous novel, **Jamaica Inn** (1936).

Henderson, and hurled him headfirst into the sea. The next wave capsized the lifeboat, trapping one man underneath it. The other two men fought their way through the swirling surf and collapsed onto the beach. With the boat still on top of him, the trapped man also reached the shore. After he kicked a hole in the wood and yelled for help, his friends rescued him.

Meanwhile, the second officer, Alexander Cook, and a boy named Kingcross attempted to swim to shore with a lifeline. The men on board the *Speke* watched with their hearts in their mouths. 'The seas were breaking clean over the ship, and we had to seek shelter in the wheelhouse or anywhere we could,' one said. 'For all we knew, the masts and rigging might come down any

> **MYSTERY FIGUREHEAD**
> The **Speke**'s figurehead was a carved wooden figure of a person, almost 3 metres tall, with long hair and flowing robes. Some people say it was supposed to represent a beautiful woman, carrying a bunch of daffodils. Others think that it was meant to be the figure of John Hanning Speke, the explorer who discovered the source of the Nile River, and that he was dressed in Egyptian clothing, holding a bundle of papyrus.

minute, but luckily nothing of the kind happened.' Cook and Kingcross did secure the rope and all the remaining sailors clung to it and worked their way to shore.

The exhausted men trudged overland until they came to Paddy Phelan's and 'The Pines'. They were taken to Cowes, where news of the *Speke*'s fate was telegraphed to Melbourne. Frank Henderson was drowned and the crew had lost everything. 'We have come away with only the clothes we stand in,' one man said. They planned to swim out to the ship at low tide the next day – if the sea calmed down – climb the rope ladder, and collect their belongings. But the rough conditions continued and it was impossible. The crew went to Melbourne to return home. An inquiry was held and Captain Tilston's master's certificate was suspended for a year because he was found guilty of poor navigation.

> Relics from the Speke ended up all over Phillip Island.

WRECKED!
The story of the Speke

> **SABOTAGE!**
> The Greenpeace ship **Rainbow Warrior** was moored in Auckland Harbour in July 1985, waiting to lead a group of peace vessels to Mururoa Atoll to protest against French nuclear testing. One night two explosions wrecked it, killing Portuguese photographer Fernando Pereira. Inquiries revealed that two French secret agents were responsible for the bombing. The French defence minister resigned and the agents were jailed, but later released.

The remains of the Speke

Powerful waves kept pounding the *Speke* against the rocks. Within days its steel hull had torn in half. Casks, deck fittings, and other wreckage were scattered all along the beach. Bill Kennon, from Cowes, paid £12 for salvage rights to the ship – which had cost £22 000 to build in 1891. He built a big, heavy barge with wood from the ship. Local men who went out in it became known as the 'suicide crew' because their task was so dangerous. They were only able to salvage 80 fathoms of chain, two anchors, and some other parts.

Relics from the *Speke* ended up all over Phillip Island. The captain's table, the top of which had been smashed, was repaired and became the dining-table at 'The Pines'. The captain's chair went to the old Isle of Wight Hotel, but was destroyed when the hotel went up in flames in the 1920s. The ship's bell was given to the Presbyterian Church in Cowes. Students from the Cowes State School restored part of the *Speke*'s figurehead in 1940. Nana kept the compass box for the rest of her life. After her death, my family gave it and the captain's table to the museum in Cowes.

Sometimes I walk around Kitty Miller's Bay to Wreck Bay, where a twisted, rusty piece of the *Speke* remains on the rocks. Another section of the wreck lies underwater, out of sight. When I go to the beach there, I try to imagine what it was like on that wild and stormy day in 1906 when the *Speke* was wrecked.

2 Batavia's Graveyard

A grisly find

A searcher named Hugh Edwards uncovered a yellow skeleton in a shallow grave on tiny Beacon Island, off the coast of Western Australia, in July 1963. Deep sword marks in the skull and bones showed that the person had been hacked to death. Who was this poor unfortunate man? Who had killed him? And why?

A fabulous cargo

The dried and battered bones belonged to Andries de Vries. He had sailed from Holland in 1628 on the *Batavia*, a magnificent wooden sailing-ship. Big for its day, it was 43 metres long, 12 metres wide, and 12 metres deep (not counting its tall masts). It had white sails and gleaming green and gold paintwork. Its figurehead was the splendid snarling lion of Holland.

The *Batavia* was carrying a fabulous cargo, including jewellery, pottery, and twelve iron-bound chests full of silver coins. Travelling with two other ships, it was bound for the town of Batavia (now called Jakarta) on the Indonesian island of Java. The coins were to buy exotic spices, such as pepper, cloves, and balsam, and other Asian goods to take back to Europe.

Andries was an enthusiastic young clerk aged about 19. He was one of more than 300 crew, soldiers and passengers on board. Trouble soon started among them after the ship left Holland. The commander, François Pelsaert, and the navigator, Adriaen Jacobsz, were old enemies. Jacobsz didn't like having Pelsaert in charge and was jealous of his friendship with the lovely Lucretia van der Mylen, a married woman sailing to Java to join her husband. While Pelsaert and Jacobsz fought, Jerome Cornelisz, the ship's third most senior officer, plotted mutiny. He got Jacobsz on side and somehow the *Batavia* became separated from the other two ships. Was this accidental, or part of the mutineers' plan?

Aground!

Pelsaert was sick in bed on the morning of 4 June 1629, when suddenly there was a loud scrape and everything around him shook violently. Strong winds had blown the ship onto a coral reef off Houtman Abrolhos, three groups of small rocky islands, about 70 kilometres from Geraldton, Western Australia. Surf swirled and hissed around the ship. The crew pushed

> **'LOOK OUT!'**
> Frederik de Houtman, a Dutch commander, discovered and named Houtman Abrolhos in 1619. 'Abrolhos' comes from a Portuguese term meaning 'Look out!' or 'Take care!'

WRECKED!
Batavia's Graveyard

the bronze cannon overboard and cut down the main mast to make the ship lighter, but the *Batavia* was well and truly stuck.

Shrieks of terror filled the air as passengers clambered over each other to get into the lifeboats. Below deck, soldiers and crew members went wild, breaking into casks of wine and brandy, and plundering the chests of coins. Forty people drowned trying to swim ashore, but the rest struggled to the islands. Pounding seas broke up the *Batavia* within a week. Cornelisz was the last person to abandon ship.

How would the castaways survive on these sandy, treeless, uninhabited islands with no fresh water? For shelter, they built makeshift tents from the ship's sails. Some had grabbed barrels of bread and water from the hold, but salt water ruined most of the water. Starving, they clubbed seals to death, captured birds and raided their nests for eggs, and caught fish. Thirst turned their tongues black, and some people died an agonising death before rain fell. Pelsaert and others searched about 160 kilometres of the coast of the mainland (now called Australia) but they could not find a river.

> ...cast away on sandy islands with no fresh water...thirst turned their tongues black

The town of Batavia was 3220 kilometres away. Pelsaert, Jacobsz, and about 30 other

Wreck of the Batavia

people set off on the hazardous trip in a small open lifeboat. They managed to reach their destination and borrow a bigger boat so that they could rescue the stranded survivors. But Jacobsz was arrested and thrown in prison for failing as a navigator and allowing the *Batavia* to hit the reef. He was also suspected of having mutinous intentions. Pelsaert made it back to the islands about three months after the ship was wrecked.

WRECKED!
Batavia's Graveyard

> **RELICS FROM THE *BATAVIA***
>
> Experts have thoroughly explored the wreck of the Batavia and have recovered many relics from it. These include cannon and cannon balls, a stone gateway, an anchor, jugs, some of the silver coins, a very rare astrolabe (a navigational instrument), and even part of the ship itself. They are now held by the Western Australian Maritime Museum.

Bloodshed

While Pelsaert was away trying to get help, Cornelisz revised his plans for mutiny. He and his 20 henchmen would steal the treasure, get rid of almost everyone else, and seize the rescue ship when it arrived. Then they would take to the high seas as pirates. They established their headquarters on a tiny island that the survivors of the wreck called Batavia's Graveyard, and put their murderous scheme into action.

They tied people up and threw them into the sea to drown. They stabbed others with knives and swords, and callously strangled babies. All in all they massacred more than 125 men, women and children on Batavia's Graveyard, and on nearby Traitor's and Seal's Islands.

Andries begged for mercy when the mutineers prepared to drown him. They let him live, but forced him to cut the throats of about 20 sick people. After that they broke Andries' shoulder, struck him over the head, and slashed his throat.

Cornelisz gave himself the grand title of 'Captain-General'. He and his collaborators strutted around their blood-soaked little island dressed in scarlet and gold outfits salvaged from the ship's cargo. They dragged women into their tents and raped them. Against her will, Lucretia had to live with Cornelisz for two months.

On another island, Webbye Hays and 40 soldiers remained loyal to Pelsaert. A handful of people who had escaped warned them about the mutiny. The Defenders (as Hays and his supporters became known) fought off two vicious attacks and managed to capture Cornelisz and kill some of his men. The mutineers who were left on Batavia's Graveyard then elected Wouter Loos to take Cornelisz's place as their leader. When Pelsaert finally returned, Hays told him of the terrible things that had happened.

'Revenge! Revenge!'

Pelsaert tortured the murderers until they confessed their crimes. Then he administered drastic punishments. Cornelisz's hands

> ...hands were cut off...

were cut off and he was hanged on Seal's Island in early October. 'Revenge! Revenge!' were his last words. On the same day, four of his men had their right hands chopped off and were also hanged.

WRECKED!
Batavia's Graveyard

A cabin boy, called Jan Pillegran de Bye, was condemned to hang, but he cried so much that Pelsaert took pity and left him with Wouter Loos on the mainland, as punishment. The two faced an unknown land. All they had were a few bells, beads and mirrors to trade with local Aboriginal people. Imagine how they must have felt as they watched the ship sail away...

Pelsaert retrieved most of the silver before setting off with the survivors for Batavia. Once there, the authorities hanged several more of the mutineers and mutilated others. Pelsaert was a shattered man and died the following year. Hays became a hero. Lucretia never saw her husband again – he had died before she reached Batavia.

A big discovery

Pelsaert wrote about the tragedy, but the exact location of the wreck remained a mystery for more than 300 years. No one even knew which island was Batavia's Graveyard. Hugh Edwards, a reporter, became determined to find the wreck.

He led a search to the islands in 1960. It was unsuccessful but he did not lose interest. Soon afterwards he heard that a local fisherman, Dave Johnson, had found an anchor in shallow water while out fishing. Johnson later returned to the same area and saw some stone blocks and a cannon under the water. In 1963 he told one of Edwards' fellow searchers of his big discovery.

Edwards and others dived on the wreck. They also dug up the bones of Andries de Vries and some of his unlucky companions on Beacon Island – which turned out to be Batavia's Graveyard.

WRECKED!

3 The mutiny on the **Bounty**

Bread-fruit and the Bounty

Forty-three men sailed from England on the Bounty in December 1787. They were going to Tahiti to collect bread-fruit plants to take to the West Indies for British planters to grow as cheap food for their slaves. It was hard for the crew not to get in each other's way because the ship was so small. It was only about 8 metres wide and 30 metres long – less than half as long as a jumbo jet.

There were two very tough men on the *Bounty*. One was the commander, the bad-tempered Lieutenant William Bligh; the other was the senior master's mate, a charismatic character named Fletcher Christian. They had sailed together on other voyages and, although Christian was only nine years younger, he was like a son to Bligh. But they argued on the way to Tahiti, probably over money.

The *Bounty* spent five months anchored off Tahiti from October 1788. The weather was warm and the beaches were beautiful. There was plenty of fresh food, and the men were settling in to life with the friendly Tahitians. No wonder they were unhappy when it came time

The Bounty

to leave. To make matters worse, there was no room to move, with 750 bread-fruit plants cluttering up the main cabin.

'Blow his brains out'

One morning about three weeks after leaving Tahiti, Fletcher Christian and some other crew members burst into Bligh's cabin

> Fletcher Christian burst into Bligh's cabin...

just before daybreak. Christian's long dark hair was all over the place, and his shirt was flapping open. He was like a wild man, waving guns and

WRECKED!
The mutiny on the *Bounty*

a cutlass. He ordered his men to drag Bligh out of bed, tie his hands behind his back, and kill him if he made a sound.

They forced Bligh up onto the deck. He was made to look ridiculous, with his nightshirt tangled up in the ropes around him, showing his bare bottom. Other men rushed up to see what was going on. Christian was going to take command of the ship! Bligh pleaded with him to stop the mutiny, but he refused.

The mutineers shoved the commander and eighteen other crew members into an open boat. When Bligh protested, one man yelled, 'Blow his brains out.' William Bligh and his unfortunate companions were allowed to take some food, canvas, sails, twine, tools, a quadrant and compasses, and four cutlasses with them. But no maps or charts! They watched helplessly as the *Bounty* sailed into the distance.

Bligh and his men reached one of the nearby Friendly (Tongan) Islands that evening. But a few nights later they heard the ominous sound of stones being clacked together. Someone was going to be killed! As they rushed back to their boat, about 200 not-so-friendly islanders gathered and began hurling large

...no maps or charts!...only a couple of pieces of bread to eat...

stones at them. One of Bligh's men was hit so hard he collapsed into the water – stone dead! The others desperately pushed the boat out to sea and tossed clothes into the water to distract their attackers. They were hurt and terrified, but they managed to get away.

Rain poured down on them day after day as they sailed towards the north coast of New Holland (now called Australia). Bligh ordered the men to soak their clothes in sea water – which was warmer than the rain – so that they didn't catch chills. Most days they only had a couple of pieces of bread to eat and a cupful of water to drink. They were so hungry they even ate the beaks and feet of seabirds that they caught, and gobbled down oysters, clams, and wild fruit when they rested on a small island that

WRECKED!
The mutiny on the Bounty

> **PANDORA'S BOX**
> The beautiful Pandora was the first woman created by the Greek gods, according to mythology. She had a box full of all kinds of evils, and when it was opened, all the horrible things flew out and plagued the world. The only thing left inside was hope. When people use the words 'Pandora's Box' they are talking about something that will cause lots of unmanageable problems once it is opened or activated.

they called Restoration Island.

The weakened and bedraggled party crawled up a beach on Timor in June, almost seven weeks after being set adrift. They had sailed 6700 kilometres in an extraordinary feat of navigation. Bligh's brilliant skills as a sailor had saved them from watery graves. Most of them returned, via Batavia (now called Jakarta), to England. But not all of them made it. Four died from fever in Timor and Batavia, one died on the way home, and one was left behind and never heard of again. The British government did not blame Bligh for the mutiny and later appointed him governor of New South Wales.

The story of the Pandora

After getting rid of Bligh, Fletcher Christian and his men dumped the hated bread-fruit plants overboard. They made a trip to Tahiti to pick up some men and women, and hundreds of pigs, and then settled on the island of Tubuai, where they built themselves a fort. The mutineers rampaged around the island, grabbing women, burning houses, and murdering people. They were lawless and unruly, and fought among themselves. Eventually they decided to leave Tubuai and split into two groups. So Christian dropped sixteen of them on Tahiti in September 1789, before sailing away with eight others on the *Bounty*.

FIJI

TONGA
(FRIENDLY ISLANDS)

TAHITI

TUBUAI ISLANDS

PITCAIRN ISLAND

NORFOLK ISLAND

--- VOYAGE OF BLIGH'S OPEN BOAT
✗ WRECK OF THE PANDORA

WRECKED!
The mutiny on the Bounty

Captain Edward Edwards, commander of the *Pandora*, was sent in search of the mutineers. In March 1791 he captured fourteen of them on Tahiti (the other two had been murdered). Edwards showed no mercy and imprisoned them in a wooden cell on the ship's deck. It became known as 'Pandora's Box'. The men were naked, except for heavy iron cuffs on their wrists and ankles. Rain poured over them through gaps in the wood. They could hear the wails of their Tahitian lovers paddling their canoes around the ship.

> ...prisoners in the cell screamed for help...

The *Pandora* left Tahiti seven or eight weeks later to keep searching the Pacific for the other mutineers. Edwards became more and more fed up. The only trace he could find of the *Bounty* was a floating piece of wood! Worse still, five of his own crew disappeared after he sent them ashore on another island. Eventually he gave up and headed for England.

Panic

But on the way, late one night in August 1791, the *Pandora* smashed into the Great Barrier Reef. The panic-stricken prisoners in the cell screamed for help. Three were dragged out to pump water from the sinking ship. The others struggled to pull off their cuffs, but Edwards told the master-at-arms to do them up again and make sure that the men were kept in the box. A huge wave, however, swept the master-at-arms into the sea.

The quarter-master's mate felt sorry for the trapped men, so he opened the hatch and tossed in the keys to the cuffs. They fought frantically to free themselves. One was too slow and drowned while still in the box. (Archaeologists found his skeleton and a half-opened padlock in the wreck.) Another drowned after jumping overboard while still handcuffed. A gangplank crashed onto two other prisoners floating in the water, and killed them.

Thirty of the *Pandora*'s crew also died that dreadful night. Ninety-nine men from the wreck, including the ten surviving prisoners, swam or drifted 4 or 5 kilometres to a cay (or sandbank), which became known as Pandora's Cay. It was tiny, about 90 metres long and 60 metres wide. Edwards put up tents made from sails for his crew, but sent the mutineers off without any protection to the other side of the sandbank. There they froze at night and burned by day. To try to protect their lily-white bodies from the fierce sun, they buried themselves up to their necks in sand.

Several days later, all the *Pandora* survivors squeezed into four small boats

WRECKED!
**The mutiny on
the** Bounty

retrieved from the ship and set off for Timor, about 1850 kilometres away. Their boats were even more overcrowded than Bligh's, and they also had little food or water. Somehow they too reached Timor. Soon they were on their way home to England on another ship. The prisoners defiantly wore jaunty straw hats that they had made themselves.

> ...the mutineers burnt the Bounty...

The ten men faced a court martial in England in September 1792. Four were found not guilty. The other six were found guilty and sentenced to death – but three of them were pardoned. The three condemned men were hanged one morning in October 1792 on a ship anchored off the English coast. Thousands of ghoulish sightseers stood on the shore and nearby ships to watch the hangings. The men's gaoler stole their nightcaps as souvenirs! Years later, in 1809, one of the pardoned men thought he saw Fletcher Christian walking along a street in England. Was this possible?

An island hideaway

Christian and the other eight mutineers landed on remote, uninhabited Pitcairn Island in January 1790. With them were twelve women, six men and a child, from Tahiti and other islands. Matthew Quintal, one of the mutineers, burnt the *Bounty* to hide their traces. The mutineers divided the land into nine parts and set up households with some of the women. For a while everything seemed fine – children were born and gardens flourished.

But violence broke out again and again over the next few years. There were murders, accidents and one suicide. Both Tahitians and mutineers died. Christian's end came in 1793, when some of the cruelly treated native men killed him and four other mutineers. When Edward Young died from asthma in 1800, he was the first mutineer on the island to die a natural death.

John Adams (known as Alexander Smith on the *Bounty*) was the only man left on Pitcairn Island. With him were nine women, a girl, and 23 children born on the island. One night he had a transforming dream, and he became very

> The rest of the world knew nothing...

religious, preaching and praying much of the time. He remained on the island until he died in 1829.

The rest of the world knew nothing about the settlement, or what happened on Pitcairn Island, until an American sea captain stumbled upon it in 1808. A few other people went to live there and more children were born. By 1856 there were about 200 Pitcairn Islanders, too many for the island's resources.

WRECKED!
The mutiny on the Bounty

So, that year, the islanders moved to Norfolk Island, which was being abandoned as a convict settlement. A few became homesick and went back to Pitcairn Island, but most stayed. On Norfolk Island they continued to use their dialect made up of a combination of English and Tahitian words. Descendants of Fletcher Christian and other *Bounty* mutineers still live on Norfolk Island today.

SOME NORFOLK ISLAND WORDS

ippy	a silly person
eyulla	acting older than they are
tin-tola	sweetheart
umer-oo-lar	clumsy
pilly-pilly	stick together
rahullo	dead banana leaf
sullun	a person
whaa	what
garit	fed up
wusser	worse
pi-ar-lee	small
semiz-wee	peculiar

4 The adventures of Eliza Fraser

The Stirling Castle

Eliza Fraser was pregnant when she boarded the Stirling Castle **in London in October 1835. Her husband, James Fraser, was the captain of the ship. They were leaving their other three children at home in the Orkney Islands.**

Five months later, the *Stirling Castle* reached Hobart Town, where it delivered cases of pale ale and collected passengers. The ship then sailed to Sydney where the rest of its cargo – ranging from pickles to rum – was unloaded and the passengers disembarked. In Sydney eleven crew members deserted, so Captain Fraser had to find replacements.

The ship, with Captain and Mrs Fraser and eighteen crew on board, left Sydney on 13 May 1836 for London via Singapore. After sailing past the notorious convict settlement of Moreton Bay (now Brisbane), it headed in the direction of the Great Barrier Reef.

Abandon ship!

One evening, about a week later, the chief officer suddenly heard sounds of surf, and in the

WRECKED!
The adventures of Eliza Fraser

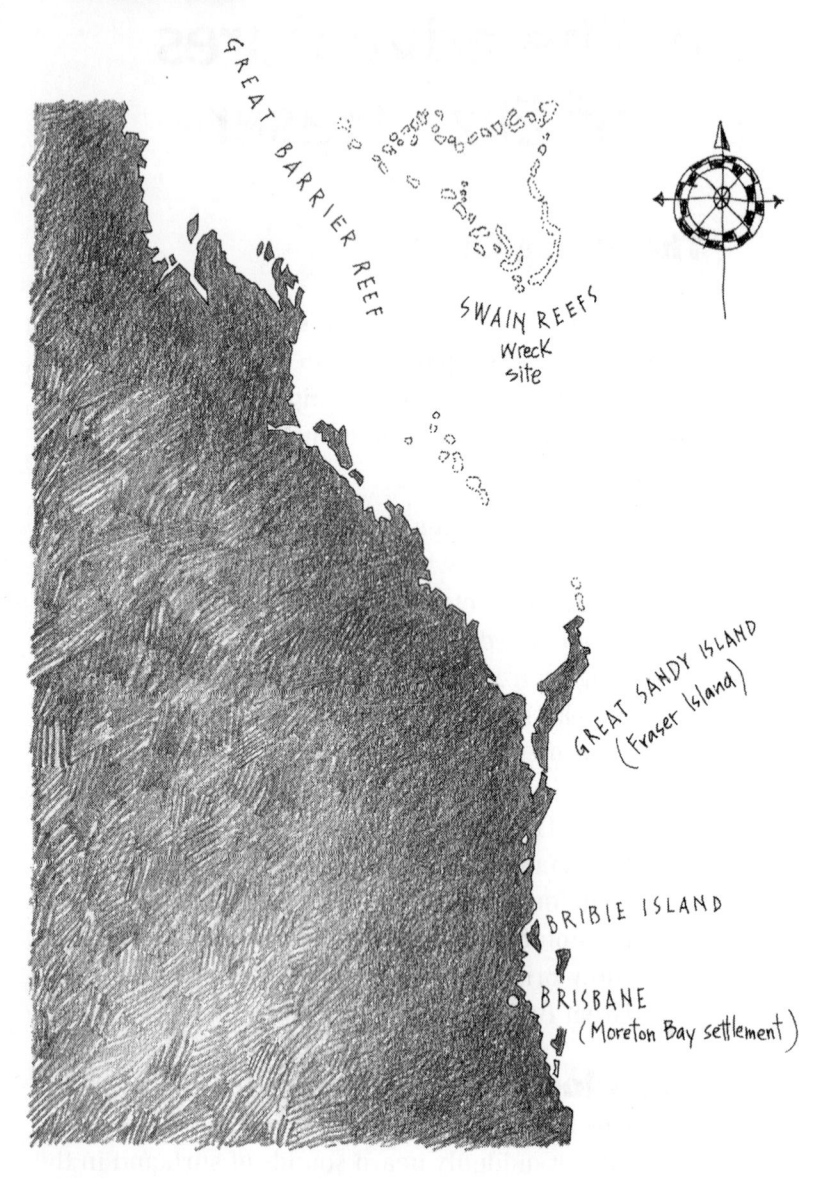

moonlight he saw waves breaking on an uncharted reef straight ahead. Before he could do anything, there was a collision and the ship was thrown on its side. Waves swept away a jolly-boat and one of the sailors. Captain Fraser emerged and began yelling orders, but they could not right the ship. The *Stirling Castle* was stuck on the reef and certain to be smashed to pieces.

> ...the long-boat was leaking badly...

The crew lowered a long-boat and a pinnace over the side. Mrs Fraser, her husband, and nine crew members clambered into the long-boat; the others into the slightly smaller pinnace. They took with them instruments and guns, three trunks of Mrs Fraser's clothes, jellies and jams for the captain (who had an ulcer), and some pale ale.

Moreton Bay, the closest white settlement, was hundreds of kilometres to the south. Could they reach it in their rickety boats, on the open sea? Each vessel had sails and oars, but the long-boat was leaking so badly that the pinnace – which was only about 8 metres long – had to tow it. Eliza Fraser, despite being pregnant, helped the crew bail water out of the leaky long-boat, but Captain Fraser was too sick to do anything. A few days later, Eliza went into labour and gave birth in the long-boat, but in the

WRECKED!
The adventures of Eliza Fraser

confusion a tragedy occurred. The baby drowned *in* the boat.

After another day or two, the party stopped briefly on a little island. Eliza Fraser climbed a cliff to collect water for her husband, while the sailors mixed sand, soap, and grease together to try to repair the holes in the boat. Then they set off again, the pinnace still towing the long-boat.

No water

For weeks they battled along. Sometimes reefs blocked their way, so they had to get out and carry the boats. They collected shellfish to eat from the reefs, but had to be careful not to step on dangerous stone-fish and sea-snakes. They were so thirsty that some of them drank sea-water, which made them horribly sick. The second mate, John Baxter, who had been in charge of the pinnace, felt so ill that he had to move and be looked after in the long-boat.

Edward Stone, the boatswain, took control of the pinnace, and he and his men went off alone to search for water. Mrs Fraser and the

> ...some of them drank sea-water...

others from the long-boat waited patiently for two days on a large rock in the middle of the ocean, but the men did not return. Stone and company had decided to try to save just themselves.

So the long-boat set off alone. For a week

> **ADRIFT AT SEA!**
> In 1973, Maurice and Maralyn Bailey were sailing their yacht Auralyn in the Pacific Ocean, near the Galapagos Islands, when it hit a whale and sank. For almost four months, they drifted in their life-raft and rubber dinghy, which were tied together. They caught fish, turtles and birds in order to survive, and made dominoes and cards to entertain themselves. Seven ships passed by in the distance before an eighth finally rescued them.

the people on board had almost no food or water. The starving men began talking about 'drawing lots' – whoever lost would be killed and eaten by the others. Fortunately, the long-boat reached land before this actually happened. They thought it was the mainland, but it was really Great Sandy Island (now Fraser Island).

Living with Aboriginal people

Groups of Aboriginal people approached them several times in the next few days, and gave them food in exchange for clothes. Captain Fraser wanted to wait for the weather to improve so that they could continue in the long-boat, but most of the crew thought it would be better to walk along the coast to Moreton Bay. 'Big Bob' Darge, Hendy Youlden, and others set off, still not knowing that they were on an island. As the weather did not change, Captain and Mrs Fraser, Baxter, and the rest followed. Eliza said that Aboriginal people, who had helped the Frasers' party find fresh water in the sand, took away their clothes,

WRECKED!
The adventures of Eliza Fraser

except for her sou'wester hat. So she made herself a skirt from sea-grape. In it she hid her wedding ring and earrings.

For the next few days, Eliza and her companions pressed on along the beach. Writers have told a story of how Aboriginal men, with clubs and spears, ambushed Captain Fraser and his men and forced them into the bush. Eliza tried to follow but was pushed away. Some Aboriginal women took her to their camp, where they fed her, covered her body with charcoal and grease, and stuck feathers in her hair.

Some weeks after Eliza began living with the Aboriginal women, she saw her husband in a clearing. He told her that all the men from the long-boat, including Darge and Youlden's group, had been captured. He asked her to help him, but some Aboriginal men appeared, so she hid behind a tree. The men were angry and, suddenly, one speared the captain through the back. Eliza rushed to pull out the spear. 'Eliza, I am gone forever!' James Fraser gasped. Blood trickled from his mouth and he died before her eyes. Horrified, Eliza fainted. When she recovered, the body had gone.

A wide and fast-flowing channel of water separated the island from the mainland. Aboriginal people took Mrs Fraser and some of the men, including 'Big Bob' Darge, across in

> ...dolphins helped him to catch fish...

their canoes, but three were left behind. Two made a desperate attempt to swim to the mainland, but they were devoured by sharks. John Baxter, the only *Stirling Castle* survivor left on the island, somehow managed to stay alive. Sometimes dolphins helped him to catch fish.

'Don't shoot, sir!'

Lieutenant Charles Otter and friends, with a convict crew, sailed from Moreton Bay in early August 1836 to go to Bribie Island on a fishing and shooting trip. While Otter was out shooting, three men suddenly stepped out of the bush in front of him. 'Don't shoot, sir! We're British subjects! Shipwrecked sailors!' one called out. They turned out to be 'Big Bob' Darge, another survivor, and an Aboriginal man who was showing them the way to Moreton Bay. They had abandoned Youlden about 40 kilometres back, because he was too weak to keep going. No one knows for certain why they were going via Bribie Island. Otter collected him and the whole party set off by boat for Moreton Bay.

News of Eliza Fraser and the other survivors reached Moreton Bay just before Otter did. Several Aboriginal people had walked hundreds of kilometres to tell their friend John Graham the story. Graham was a convict who had escaped from Moreton Bay in 1827 and lived with Aboriginal people until 1833, when he gave himself up. Although still serving his sentence,

WRECKED!
The adventures of Eliza Fraser

he was acting as a constable looking after other convicts. He immediately offered to go and rescue the survivors – if he succeeded he might be made a free man.

Otter, two other soldiers, Graham, and thirteen convict volunteers left Moreton Bay in whaling boats on 11 August. Within days, Graham found two survivors near the Noosa River, John Baxter on Great Sandy Island, and Mrs Fraser, also on the mainland. When Graham found her, Eliza looked like a skeleton. She was still wearing the sou'wester. On the boat trip back to Moreton Bay she collapsed into a fever.

> ...Eliza looked like a skeleton...

In the meantime, 'Middle Bob' Hodge, a survivor from the pinnace, had reached Sydney by boat after being found on the coast near Port Macquarie. He made up an innocent-sounding story about how the pinnace and long-boat had become separated. After reaching the mainland, he and his party had begun walking south. They missed Moreton Bay. Hodge told a story of misery, with two of the men drowning, two being speared, one collapsing in the bush, and the remaining one, he claimed, being burnt and eaten by Aboriginal people.

The *Prince George* was sent from Sydney to Moreton Bay to pick up Mrs Fraser, Baxter, and the five other long-boat survivors. On its way back to Sydney, it stopped in the area where Hodge had been found to check whether anyone else from the pinnace had survived. Only one headless body, identified by its waistcoat, was found. It was lying in the remains of a fire. Wild dogs – or Hodge, some people believed – had eaten parts of the legs.

Eliza becomes famous

After her arrival in Sydney, Eliza was made a celebrity. The people of Sydney donated hundreds of pounds to assist her and she attended countless picnics and parties. In February 1837, two days before sailing from Sydney for England on a ship called the *Mediterranean Packet*, she secretly married its captain, Alexander Greene. The ship reached Liverpool in July 1837.

Still hiding her new marriage, Eliza pleaded for money from authorities in Liverpool and London. She told strange and fabulous tales about her experiences, for example, that her Aboriginal captors had blue hair growing out of their shoulders and from the middle of their heads, and that on one occasion Aboriginal women had saved her from the grip of a boa constrictor. Later, she became an attraction in a show in London.

Eliza, her three children, and Captain Greene eventually migrated to New Zealand.

WRECKED!
The adventures of Eliza Fraser

She is thought to have died in a carriage accident in Australia in 1858. Her story lives on in books, paintings, and a film.

5 Australia's worst shipwreck

Farewell to the old world

The Cataraqui **set sail from the English port of Liverpool in April 1845. It was bound for Melbourne, Australia, on the other side of the world. On board were 367 migrants from England and Ireland, many of whom were related to each other. There were more than 60 families among them. Almost half were children, aged 14 or younger. Another four babies were born during the voyage.**

A lot of the families came from neighbouring villages. Some parts of Britain had become very overcrowded, and there were not enough jobs to go around. Most of the migrants were poor, so they had decided to make new lives for themselves in a faraway country.

They looked forward to a land of new opportunities. They hoped to find work, better food and even the chance to own their own land. But first they had to endure a long and dangerous voyage.

> ...four babies were born during the voyage...

WRECKED!
Australia's worst shipwreck

Batten down the hatches!

Few of the people leaving had ever seen the sea before they stepped onto the *Cataraqui*. The three-masted wooden sailing ship was only 42 metres long by 9 metres wide. It was a reasonable size for its time but very small compared with modern ships. The *Cataraqui* reached Cape Town, at the southern tip of Africa, by the end of June.

The powerful winds known as the 'roaring forties' blew the little ship on its way again. Like other ships in those days, it roughly followed the 40 degrees south latitude. It battled huge waves and had to dodge dangerous icebergs. Wild storms lashed the *Cataraqui* during the first two weeks of the voyage in July. The crew battened down the hatches, leaving all the passengers crammed together down below. With no room to move and not enough fresh air, people suffered horribly from claustrophobia and seasickness, and some of the babies died.

> ...huge waves and dangerous icebergs ...no lighthouses to mark the way...

Captain Christopher William Finlay had to find the narrow entry to Bass Strait – 'thread-the-eye-of-the-needle' – between the rugged Otway coast and hard-to-see King Island. This was difficult at the best of times and the bad weather made it much harder. In those days sailors used the sun and stars to navigate. But as the

Restored remains of the Speke's **figurehead**

The Loch Ard Peacock

Iron spike and latch – relics from the Mahogany Ship?

Relics?

For over one hundred years searchers have attempted to locate and identify the wreck. This bronze spike and oven latch were located during an expedition in the 1890's and were originally thought to have come from the *Mahogany Ship*.

The search continues for the tangible evidence which will once and for all establish the *Mahogany Ship's* place in Australian history.

The wreck of the Batavia

The Great Barrier Reef – a hidden danger for ships

The replica of the Bounty sails daily on Sydney Harbour

Australia 33c
Terra Australis:
Coastal Shipwrecks
Astrolabe
Batavia 1629

Modern stamp showing the astrolabe from the *Batavia*

Eliza Fraser

Eva Carmichael

Tom Pearce

Cataraqui sailed into Australian waters, dark storm clouds hid the stars. There were no lighthouses to mark the way in this area, although the colonists had been urgently calling for them to be built.

A furious storm raged on the evening of Sunday, 3 August 1845, as the captain tried to find his way. He thought he was close to the

The treacherous rocks of King Island

WRECKED!
Australia's worst shipwreck

mainland, around Portland, heading towards Cape Otway. In the midst of the storm, he slowed the ship down by 'heaving to' – turning it into the wind with few sails up. Everything seemed to calm down at about 3 am the next morning, so he decided to move on. But the ship was really about 185 kilometres south of where the captain believed it to be. And it was dangerously close to King Island.

Jagged reefs

The *Cataraqui* crashed onto the jagged reefs off the western coast of King Island at about 4.30 am on Monday, 4 August. Twice more it smashed onto the rocks, ending up on its side. Crew members frantically hacked down the masts hoping to right the ship, but that failed. Below decks the passengers were thrown from their beds, children were screaming in terror, and all their belongings were tossed about.

When day broke they could see the beach – about 140 metres away. But they might just as well have been 140 kilometres away.

THE MARITIME GRAVEYARD

King Island used to be known as the 'maritime graveyard of Bass Strait' because so many ships were wrecked around its shores. Some people say that the high quality of the grasses grown from straw mattresses washed ashore is the main reason why the island's dairy products are excellent.

The waves were enormous and there were few gaps in the reefs. Lifeboats were washed away or capsized. Ropes thrown towards the shore became tangled in kelp and seaweed. For the next two days men, women and children clung to each other and to the ship, but wave after wave swept them away. Most of the passengers had never learned to swim. Even those who could stood little chance against the rocks. Eventually the *Cataraqui* slipped under the water. Four hundred lives were lost.

> **Four hundred lives were lost.**

Somehow nine bedraggled men got ashore: eight crew members, including Thomas Guthery, who was second in command of the ship, and one migrant, named Solomon Brown. They were in a pitiful state when they reached the shore on Tuesday, 5 August. They were naked, battered and bruised from the rocks, and had no food or water. They had no idea where they were. Scattered along the beach for as far as they could see were the bodies of their shipmates, torn apart by rocks and sea. The exhausted group scrambled into nearby bush and collapsed. How would they survive?

Search and rescue

King Island was officially uninhabited, but fortunately there were four people on the island at the time. Two Aboriginal people called Maria and

WRECKED!
Australia's worst shipwreck

Georgia were living there. David Howie and another man had been dropped there at the beginning of August to spend three months hunting kangaroos and wallabies for their skins. The two women helped them with their work. Howie was a former convict who had been transported to Van Diemen's Land (now Tasmania) in 1837 for theft or receiving stolen goods. A few years later he was given a free certificate. The men had a camp at Yellow Rock, north of the place where the *Cataraqui* had been wrecked.

When Howie saw a corpse and a couch floating past, he realised that there had been a shipwreck. He quickly organised a search. On the morning of Wednesday, 6 August, he found the nine survivors. They were too sick to move, so he rushed back to Yellow Rock for flour, sugar and other supplies for them. He returned to the site of the wreck in two days.

The group was stranded on the island for the time being. Howie had only a small dinghy and no way of reaching either the Port Phillip District (now Victoria) or Van Diemen's Land. It would be at least another two months

> ...the survivors were too sick to move...

before a ship called in to the island to collect him. So the survivors had to stay at the grisly site. As there was only one spade on the entire island, they could do little to bury the putrid bodies around them.

Just in case any ships visited the island while he was tending to the survivors, Howie left a note on the door of his hut at Yellow Rock, explaining what had happened. More storms forced a ketch called the *Governor Gawler* to come in and shelter off King Island, near Yellow Rock, around Friday, 8 August. Twelve days later the ketch sailed away. No one had seen the note!

About a month after the *Cataraqui* struck the reef, a little boat named the *Midge* called in at Yellow Rock. The two sailors aboard did find the message and set off to pick up the survivors. They found them on 7 September. Two days later the *Midge* left King Island for Melbourne with the survivors, David Howie and his assistant on board. The group took documents that had been washed ashore – 35 letters and two bundles of the migrants' character references.

The people of Melbourne – then only a small town ten years old – anxiously waited for word of the *Cataraqui*. The ship was overdue... Then the tragic news spread rapidly after the *Midge*'s arrival on the morning of Saturday, 13 September. A special issue of the *Port Phillip Herald* was published. A theatre performance was later held to raise money for the survivors.

Burials and memorials

David Howie told the superintendent of the Port Phillip District, Charles La Trobe, that he would go back to King Island and bury the bodies of the

WRECKED!
Australia's worst shipwreck

shipwreck victims for £50. La Trobe agreed and Howie set off by boat at the end of September 1845, with a man called Alexander Sutherland. Sutherland had paid £86 for the rights to salvage the *Cataraqui*. They almost didn't make it. Caught in the wild seas of Bass Strait, their boat drifted helplessly for almost a week, but eventually they reached the island.

Collecting the decaying remains was a ghastly task. Howie buried the bodies of 342 migrants in five big graves during the following months. He bought a small boat with his earnings and became a special constable for King Island. Sutherland had expected to make £800 by salvaging the wreck but the venture failed. He managed to sell some wood, which was used in the building of St Peter's Church, Eastern Hill, in Melbourne, but went broke and was gaoled in 1846. A wooden and iron memorial was placed on the beach at the site of the wreck in about 1848.

After the *Cataraqui* was wrecked, the British Admiralty banned ships from taking the Bass Strait route, but many captains ignored the ban because they did not want to travel the extra distance south of Van Diemen's Land. People blamed the authorities for the disaster, because there were no lighthouses to guide ships through the entry to Bass Strait. As a result of the tragedy, lighthouses were built at Cape Otway and on King Island. Workmen hacked their way through rough bush to Cape Otway and began work on a lighthouse in 1846. Its light operated from 1848 to 1994. A massive, 44-metre lighthouse was built at Cape Wickham on the northern point of King Island. It began operating in 1861.

> As a result lighthouses were built...

Cape Otway lighthouse

WRECKED!
Australia's worst shipwreck

Cape Wickham lighthouse

56

THE PHAROS OF ALEXANDRIA

The Pharos of Alexandria, a lighthouse on an island near the Egyptian city of Alexandria, was built in about 280 BC. It was one of the seven wonders of the ancient world and became the model for all lighthouses built since then. The Pharos was a stone tower with three storeys. The bottom one was square, the middle one octagonal, and the highest one round, with a huge statue above it. A wood fire was lit in the top storey at night. Its light, which was reflected by a number of mirrors, could be seen 67 kilometres away. Some people believed that the mirrors could destroy enemy ships approaching Alexandria! Part of the Pharos was destroyed by an earthquake in about 1100AD, the remainder by another earthquake in the 1400s.

STOP PRESS

September 1995: Archaeologists announced that they had discovered the remains of the Pharos among underwater ruins. Some of the huge stone blocks they found are estimated to weigh up to 75 tonnes each. Divers soon recovered six monuments from the watery site, including a one-tonne sphinx and a headless statue of the pharaoh, Ramses II. How do you think that these ruins could have ended up on the seabed?

WRECKED!
Australia's worst shipwreck

Gale force winds and raging seas had claimed the lives of 400 people from the *Cataraqui* in August 1845. Later storms destroyed the original memorial to them. Another memorial, a small cairn, was erected on the beach in 1956. But the most meaningful memorials to those people, the victims of Australia's worst shipwreck, were the lighthouses constructed on Cape Otway and Cape Wickham. Over the years they have guided countless other ships safely into Bass Strait. But even they have not been able to save all of the ships that have tried to enter that treacherous stretch of water.

6 Eva's story

A new life

Eva Carmichael was excited. So were all the other people attending the farewell party on board the Loch Ard. **It was the evening of Friday, 31 May 1878, and the thirteen-week voyage from England was almost over. Soon the three-masted iron sailing-ship would reach Melbourne, the capital of the booming colony of Victoria.**

When 18-year-old Eva went to bed that night her head was probably filled with thoughts about her new life. She and her family had left Ireland and were going to live in Queensland. Eva's father, Dr Evory Carmichael, had tuberculosis and hoped that the new climate would improve his health. He had worked as the ship's doctor on the way out. Eva's mother, eldest sister, Raby, two little sisters, Meta and Annie, and two of her brothers, Evory and Thomas, were also on board. Only her brother William was missing – he had run away to sea after fighting with their father.

Looming cliffs

While Eva slept, the ship sailed along in heavy fog. But Captain George Gibb was becoming worried. He had expected to see the reassuring beam from the Cape Otway lighthouse at 3 am

WRECKED!
Eva's story

on Saturday morning, but there was no sign of it.

> The *Loch Ard* **was way off course...**

Soon after, the haze cleared and he could see rugged cliffs less than 2 kilometres away. The sound of breaking waves could be heard. The *Loch Ard* was way off course.

Captain Gibb fought frantically to save his ship from hitting the looming cliffs. First he tried to swing it around and head out to sea, but could not get enough wind into the sails. So he ordered the crew to drop two anchors overboard. Fifty fathoms (about 90 metres) of chain rattled over with them, but the anchors dragged along the smooth, sandy seabed. The *Loch Ard* drifted rapidly towards a small island just off the coast. Once more the captain tried to sail out to sea, and the *Loch Ard* began to turn – but it was too late.

A 'fearful shuddering crash'

The ship's wooden yard-arms smashed into the cliffs of the island. Again and again powerful waves hurled the *Loch Ard* against the rock face. Large chunks of limestone fell onto the decks. Then, with a 'fearful shuddering crash' the ship hit a reef. The

> **'...I died like a sailor'**

wooden top deck ripped away from the ship's iron hull. Masts and rigging toppled, crushing two men. One died instantly, and they were both swept overboard.

Water flooded into the cabins, trapping some people. The ship had only six lifebelts for all the 54 crew and passengers on board. Dr Carmichael grabbed the lifebelts. He and his wife, Raby and Eva, and two other passengers struggled into them. Meta and Annie were clinging to their mother but Eva's two brothers were caught in another part of the ship.

Eva and Raby scrambled up to the deck. There, Captain Gibb shook Eva's hand and said to her, 'If you are saved, Eva, let my dear wife know that I died like a sailor.' The captain had only been married for six weeks before the *Loch Ard* sailed from England. The two sisters held hands, but a huge wave ripped them apart and hurled them into the sea.

Icy water

Eva floundered in the icy water. 'One of the strings attached to my lifebelt broke, and the belt, shifting up and down, forced

> The captain went down with the ship...

my head under several times, which almost cost me my life,' she later said. Eva couldn't swim but somehow she managed to clutch onto a chicken coop that was floating past. Another passenger, Arthur Mitchell, also took hold of it. By this time the *Loch Ard* had sunk, only ten or fifteen minutes after striking the reef. The captain was among those who went down with the ship.

WRECKED!
Eva's story

> **TREASURE TROVE!**
> Treasure seekers and archaeologists have always been curious to discover lost ships. Year after year, Belgian diver Robert Sténuit pored over dusty old documents, trying to work out the location of the Girona, a heavily laden Spanish galleon that sank off the Irish coast in 1588. His dreams came true in 1967, when he finally located the wreck. Over the next two years, he and his team recovered more than 12 000 objects from it, including hundreds of gold and silver coins, gold chains, and valuable jewellery. Their prize discovery was a gorgeous ruby-studded gold salamander pendant.
>
> **Ruby-studded salamander pendant**

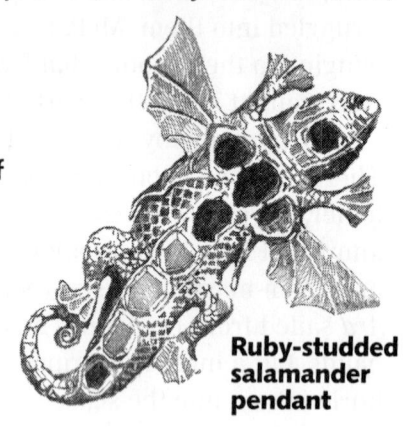

After a while, Eva and her companion let go of the coop and grabbed a floating spar. They were joined by another passenger, Reg Jones, who had had a premonition during the trip that he would never land in Victoria. The two men eventually tried to swim to shore, but they soon disappeared.

MUTTON BIRD ISLAND

LOCH ARD GORGE

> **DISCOVERY OF THE WRECK**
> In 1967 local divers discovered the wreck in about 23 metres of water, not far from Mutton Bird Island. Some items have been salvaged and are on public display in Warrnambool and Port Campbell. Others have been stolen.

Eva hung on desperately. Strong currents swept her into a long, narrow gorge, surrounded by 90-metre-high cliffs. The spar caught on the sharp edge of a cliff and Eva looked up in early morning light. Everywhere, wreckage bobbed about in the water. Then she saw a man on a little beach at the end of the gorge. Eva yelled for help.

The man was Tom Pearce, an apprentice

63

WRECKED!
Eva's story

from Melbourne. He was also aged 18. Tom and other crew members had released a lifeboat from the sinking ship but it capsized when it hit the water. He was trapped under it for three-quarters of an hour, before struggling out. He held on as the boat drifted into the gorge, where the swell of the sea turned it up the right way. Tom swam ashore through the wreckage and fell exhausted in a cave.

Rescue

When he heard Eva's cries, Tom swam out to her. She still was gripping the spar but was barely conscious by the time he reached her. Tom seized her nightdress between his teeth and dragged her through the water. It took almost an hour to rescue her. He found another cave, and rubbed some brandy onto Eva's body to revive her. She was very cold because she had been in the water for about five hours. Tom made a bed from grass and shrubs, and they both slept.

> She was barely conscious...

Some time during Saturday afternoon Tom clambered up the cliffs. He didn't know that there were steps cut into the cliff face so he went the hard way. His boots were lost and his feet hurt. Fortunately he met George Ford and William Till from Glenample station. Tom told them his terrible tale, then headed back to the beach.

Ford and Till galloped back to the station and gabbled out the story to the manager, Hugh

Gibson. Darkness had fallen by the time Gibson, Ford and Till could cover the 6 kilometres to the gorge. But Eva was no longer in the cave. Gibson stumbled around in the dark calling 'Cooee'. Poor Tom collapsed. Till went back to the station for more help, and returned with extra men, equipped with lanterns and a buggy.

Finally Ford discovered Eva crouching under a bush. She had been terrified when she woke and discovered Tom had gone. When she heard Gibson's calls, she thought they were Aboriginal war cries. The men lit a fire on the beach and gave Eva coffee and Tom some food. They carried Eva up the cliff and took her by horse and buggy to Glenample station. She stayed there for about two months, recovering from her ordeal.

Searching for bodies

Hugh Gibson found the bodies of Mrs Carmichael and Raby on Sunday. Both were still wearing their lifebelts. The following day the naked bodies of Mitchell and Jones were also found. Coffins were made for the four of them from piano cases that had been washed ashore, and they were buried on the cliff top above the gorge. Another body later washed ashore and was buried on the beach.

Searchers could see battered bodies floating along the coast during the next few days but were unable to retrieve them because the seas were

WRECKED!
Eva's story

too rough. At night a weird, purplish glow shone from a nearby blowhole. Frightened observers peered over the edge, and to their horror saw eleven bodies floating in it. The strange glow was caused by phosphorus from a case of wax matches from the wreck.

> Coffins were made from piano cases...

Salvaging the wreckage

Pianos, concertinas, clothing, candles, champagne, and other objects from the ship's cargo piled up on the beach in the gorge. Next day the beach was covered with wreckage 3 metres high, but a raging storm later carried much of it out to sea. Within days, hundreds of sightseers travelled to the area, and people grabbed whatever goods they could find.

The *Loch Ard*'s cargo was very valuable – it was valued at £53 000. A Mr J Miller paid £2120 for the rights to salvage the wreck. He arranged for the steamer *Napier* to visit the area three times, but it too was wrecked on the way back to Port Campbell. The only thing of real value that Mr Miller recovered from the *Loch Ard* was a large porcelain peacock.

Tom and Eva

Tom became a hero, showered with medals, money and other gifts. Many Victorians hoped that he would marry Eva, but three months after the *Loch Ard* was wrecked, Eva left Melbourne by steamer – she refused to get back on to a sailing ship – to return to Ireland. Tom was at the wharf to say goodbye.

Eva married an Irish man named Thomas Townshend in 1884, moved to England, and raised three sons. She died in 1934. Tom married the sister of another *Loch Ard* apprentice who had died when the ship was wrecked. Tom died in 1908.

Eva's only surviving brother,

WRECKED!
Eva's story

> **THE LOCH ARD PEACOCK**
> The porcelain peacock from the Loch Ard became famous. This exotic-looking, brightly coloured bird stands about 1.5 metres high. Made by Minton Potteries in England, the peacock was coming to Melbourne especially to appear in an exhibition. It had been carefully packed into its case and given to the captain to look after during the voyage. Amazingly it survived the wreck and only its beak was slightly damaged. The Miller family owned it until 1975. It now is displayed at the Flagstaff Hill Maritime Village in Warrnambool.

William, the one who had run away to sea, visited the gorge in 1879 and placed a headstone to the memory of the rest of the family above Mrs Carmichael and Raby's graves. It still stands in the little cemetery high above the place that is now known as Loch Ard Gorge, on the rugged south-west coast of Victoria.

7 'Grace Darling of the West'

A memorable story

When I was at school, we had class readers, which were full of stories, poems and pictures. One particular story stuck in my mind. It was called 'A Brave Australian Girl' and was about Grace Bussell, who grew up near Cape Leeuwin, in Western Australia, last century.

One day in December 1876, when Grace was aged 16, she and Sam Isaacs, an Aboriginal stockman, were out on their horses looking for missing cattle when they saw a grounded ship in the distance. It was only a few hundred metres out to sea, but heavy surf was preventing the people on board from reaching safety.

The ship was the *Georgette*, a small steamship, which was sailing south around the coast from Fremantle, carrying 58 crew and passengers and a heavy cargo of timber. Soon after setting off, it began leaking very badly. The crew tried to pump the water out, but the pumps failed and water was flooding the hull. In desperation, the captain decided to run the ship ashore.

> ...the pumps failed

WRECKED!
'Grace Darling of the West'

Tragedy struck when one lifeboat was smashed up and the eight people in it were thrown into the sea and drowned. The occupants in another lifeboat were luckier and managed to row ashore. Meanwhile the *Georgette* drifted towards land. Its boiler fires had gone out so it had really run out of steam, and its sails flapped uselessly. Finally it ran aground.

What could Grace and Sam do to help? They galloped their horses down the hill to the beach and rode straight into the water. Grace hung on grimly when her horse tripped on a line put down by the crew. They coaxed their horses out as far as they could towards the stricken ship, which was beginning to break up.

Half-drowning people clung to Grace and

Half-drowning people clung to their horses...

WRECKED!
'Grace Darling of the West'

Sam and their horses as they returned to the shore. Again and again the two riders went back into the surging seas. When all the survivors were safely ashore, Grace galloped back to her family's farm, about 13 kilometres away, for more help. Her sister and other members of the family rushed to assist the shipwreck victims.

Grace became a heroine. The British Government gave her a gold watch, and the

---

A 'VICTORIAN SUPERSTAR'

The original Grace Darling, born in 1815, was another shipwreck heroine. Her father was the keeper of the Longstone lighthouse on the Farne Islands, off the British coast.

In 1838, she took part in a notable rescue when a luxury steamship, called the Forfarshire, collided with a big rock, more than a kilometre from the lighthouse. Many people drowned, but a few survivors managed to get on to the rock. At dawn, Grace and her father saw them in the distance. They jumped into their little rowboat and headed for the rock. There they found eight men and one woman still alive. Grace stayed with the injured while her father took one group back to the lighthouse, before returning for the rest.

She was made into a 'Victorian superstar'. The Royal Humane Society awarded her a gold medal. Countless stories were written about her, and lots of 'Grace Darling' souvenirs were sold.

Royal Humane Society awarded her a silver medal, and Sam a bronze medal, for bravery. Grace, who lived until 1935, was often called the 'Grace Darling of the West'.

A MODERN SUPERSTAR

In June 1988, Kay Cottee sailed triumphantly into Sydney Harbour in her 12-metre-long yacht, First Lady. She had just become the first woman to sail solo, non-stop, and unassisted around the world, covering 25 000 nautical miles in 189 days. Cottee was named Australian of the Year for 1988.

WRECKED!

8 The Bermagui mystery

An empty boat

William Johnston was riding his horse along the beach near Corunna Point on the New South Wales coast, about 15 kilometres north of Bermagui. It was Sunday afternoon, 10 October 1880. Suddenly he came to a halt. There, on a rocky reef usually covered by water at high tide, was a small green fishing boat – with holes bashed in its sides. Something was definitely amiss. He looked around, but there was no one in sight.

Johnston was very uneasy so he went and got his friend, Albert Reed, and the two men explored the boat. They found rocks, a few bags, and other odds and ends, including a geology book belonging to someone called Lamont Young. Early next morning Reed reported their discovery to local police at the Montreal goldfields, about 6 kilometres north of Bermagui.

Henry Keightley, the mining warden from Montreal, and Senior Constable John Berry examined the boat. It was about 7 metres long and its mast, sail and paddles were tied to the seats. In the bags, clothes, books and papers were all jumbled together. There was also a sack of potatoes. Someone had been sick near the

> ...no bloodstains or signs of fighting....

bow, but there were no bloodstains or obvious signs of fighting. Some bullets were found, including one wedged in the wood of the boat. They might have been used as sinkers for the fishing-lines on board...or for a more sinister purpose. But Keightley thought that the people on board had drowned.

Five missing men

Five men were missing. One was Lamont Young, an English geologist who worked for the New South Wales mines department. He was a reliable married man, with two children and a third on the way. As part of his work, he inspected goldfields and sometimes explored

WRECKED!
The Bermagui mystery

caves. A reward of £10 was offered for the recovery of his body.

Young and his assistant, Max Schneider, had come to inspect the Montreal goldfields. Schneider was a German man with a distinctive scar on his left cheek, and he was also listed as missing. Hundreds of men – including some known criminals – had flocked to the Montreal goldfields following reports of gold discoveries. Young and Schneider arrived at Bermagui on Friday, 8 October, and set up their tent at Barter's Hole, on the Bermagui River.

The next day they walked to the goldfields. Schneider left after lunch to return to Barter's Hole, but Young stayed longer. He left some of his tools with Keightley, the warden, and told him that he probably would move his camp there on Monday. Young also said that he wanted to visit some other goldfields near Corunna Point. Before leaving Montreal, he arranged a fishing trip with Senior Constable Berry for Sunday. Young was last seen walking in the direction of Barter's Hole at about 6 pm on Saturday, 9 October.

Also missing were Thomas Towers, who owned the boat, William Lloyd, and Daniel Casey. They had sailed south from their home town, Batemans Bay, to visit the goldfields and sell potatoes to the diggers. After arriving at Bermagui on Thursday, 7 October, they moored their boat near Barter's Hole. They were experienced sailors and respectable men, although Casey sometimes got drunk.

The little green fishing-boat left the river and sailed north early on Sunday. A boy who saw it at about 7.30 am later said that there were at least four people on board. Further up the coast, Keightley saw it continuing on its way at about 10.45 am. According to Casey's son, the three men had agreed to drop Young and Schneider off at Corunna Point on their way home to Batemans Bay. The boat reached the point, but where were the men?

> The boat reached the point, but where were the men?

Searches and clues

Official and private searches discovered lots of clues. Someone had obviously gone through the men's belongings. Young's tent and some of his equipment were missing. Remains of a fire and a meal – bread, butter, damper, and an empty salmon tin – were found on the shore. Close by were a pipe, believed to belong to Schneider, and three cigar butts. There were signs that the meal had been interrupted. An axe and a shovel were found in a little bay nearby and a knife was found on the beach. A piece of shirt, thought to be Lloyd's, washed ashore. So did some gory entrails – but they turned out to be from a bullock!

The rocks in the boat had come from a

WRECKED
The Bermagui mystery

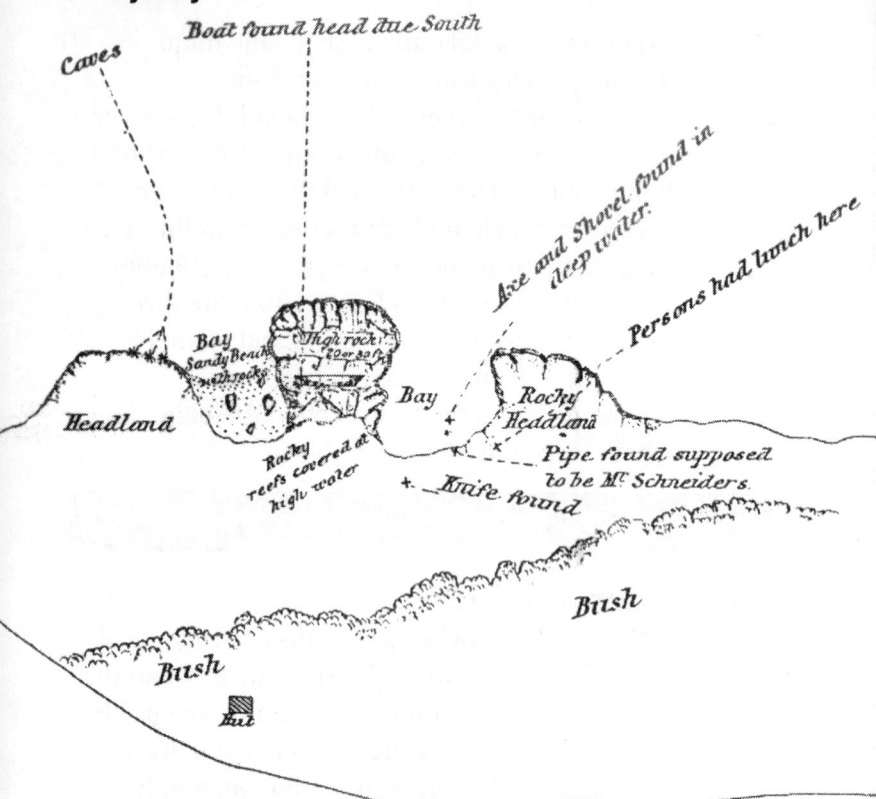

Sketch of the scene

Labels on sketch: Caves; Boat found head due South; Axe and Shovel found in deep water; Persons had lunch here; Bay Sandy Beach Wreck; High rock 20 or 30 ft; Bay; Rocky Headland; Headland; Rocky reefs covered at high water; Pipe found supposed to be Mr Schneiders; Knife found; Bush; Bush; Hut

spot about 140 metres away. No similar ones could be found anywhere else along that stretch of coast. An expert sailor said that they must have been put there after the boat reached its resting place, because it would have been too dangerous to try to land with heavy rocks and potatoes on board. He thought that the way the

> ...they didn't find a trace of the five missing men

boat was facing indicated that people were in it when it landed. If it had been empty it would have been smashed to smithereens on rocks in the water.

Searchers combed the coast in both directions. They even blasted rocks apart with dynamite in case any bodies were hidden. But they didn't find a trace of the five missing men. The government offered a reward of £50 for information about the men's disappearance and another £150 for information leading to the capture and conviction of the murderers if foul play had occurred. Young's father later added an extra £100 reward.

Was there foul play?

Henry Keightley still believed that the men had drowned. He thought the boat had probably hit a submerged rock and that those on board had been swept out to sea. But some of the men were strong swimmers. Why would they have drowned? And if they had, why had their bodies not been washed ashore? How had the boat come to be on the reef? How had the rocks got into it? And who had been eating the meal on the beach?

Keightley thought that Schneider had not been in the boat with Young and the three other men. He guessed that Schneider was left behind

WRECKED!
The Bermagui mystery

Metropolitan Police.
£300 Reward.
AUSTRALIA.

Disappeared on 9th October, 1880, five persons:—

MR. LAMONT YOUNG,
Government Geologist.

MR. MAX SCHNEIDER,
and three boatmen named

CASEY, TOWERS, and LLOYD.

They embarked in a boat at BERMAGUI, COAST OF NEW SOUTH WALES, 180 MILES SOUTH OF SYDNEY; the boat has been found jammed on the rocks at CORUNNA POINT, ten miles to the Northward; bullet marks were in the boat, but there was no trace of any struggle or foul play.

IT IS BELIEVED THE PARTY were kidnapped, and taken AWAY IN SOME VESSEL.

The sum of £100 will be paid by Major-General Young to any person giving the earliest information leading to the discovery of Mr. Lamont Young, and the Government of New South Wales will pay the Reward of £200 for such information as shall lead to the conviction of any person or persons who have been guilty of violence. Information to the COMMISSIONER OF POLICE, GREAT SCOTLAND YARD, LONDON.

E. Y. W. HENDERSON,
Commissioner of Police of the Metropolis.

Metropolitan Police Office,
4, Whitehall Place,
28th February, 1881.

HARRISON AND SONS, PRINTERS IN ORDINARY TO HER MAJESTY, ST. MARTIN'S LANE.

Police reward poster

to look after Young's tent and equipment and had fled with them when he heard that Young was missing. But why? Other people, including Young's father, were also suspicious of Schneider. Some years later, in 1887, Sydney police circulated his photo at home and abroad and there were many 'sightings' of him, but none was ever proved genuine.

If they hadn't drowned, what else could have happened to the missing men? During gold rushes, sailors often deserted and headed for the goldfields. Desperate captains sometimes, it was said, 'crimped' (kidnapped) other men to take their places. But could kidnappers have managed to take these four or five strong men? The police questioned and cleared the captain of a ketch, called the *Magic*, that had been moored in the Bermagui River at the same time as the fishing-boat. But Young's father, a Major General, became obsessed with the idea that his son had been kidnapped. No other explanation made sense to him.

An unsolved mystery

Other people, including the members of an 1883–84 government committee, were convinced that the missing men had been murdered. With a huge increase in the local population, and men frantically competing for gold, it was almost impossible to control the goings-on at the goldfields. There were reports of shady

WRECKED!
The Bermagui mystery

A GHOST SHIP – THE *MARY CELESTE*

One of the most famous unsolved mysteries of the sea involves the Mary Celeste. A crew member of another ship, the Dei Gratia, saw it sailing erratically in the Atlantic Ocean, between the Azores and Portugal, one day in December 1872. It seemed to be in trouble so the Dei Gratia sailed towards it. Something peculiar was going on – there was no one at the wheel or on the deck. The Dei Gratia's captain yelled out an offer of help, but there was no reply.

Three men from the Dei Gratia boarded and searched the Mary Celeste. There was no one on board at all. But pipes and other personal items were lying about and there was plenty of food and water. The cargo of hundreds of barrels of alcohol seemed almost untouched – only a few barrels were empty or damaged. The last entry on a chart was dated 7 November. The ship's navigational instruments, compass, and lifeboats were missing. The Dei Gratia's crew sailed the Mary Celeste to Gibraltar, and received a reward for saving the ship.

Ten people were on board the Mary Celeste when it sailed from New York for Genoa in November 1872. No trace of them has ever been found and the mystery of the Mary Celeste has never been solved. There are all sorts of theories about what happened, such as, the Mary Celeste hit a giant squid or water spout and the people on board abandoned ship and perished, or, fungus in the bread drove the people mad and made them do crazy things, causing their own deaths. What do you think?

> **THE BERMUDA TRIANGLE**
> Many strange and extraordinary things have happened in the Bermuda Triangle, an area of ocean between Bermuda and Florida. Dozens of ships and planes, and hundreds of people, have disappeared there, without a trace, since the 1940s. Were they abducted by UFOs, dragged into space-time warps by forces from long-lost civilisations, or just the victims of unfortunate accidents?

characters seen in the area at the time the men disappeared, and a suggestion that one had a scarred face.

One view was that the murderers had killed their victims at Barter's Hole, dumped their bodies at sea, and sailed on to Corunna Point, where they ransacked the boat, ate part of a meal, and put rocks in the boat to sink it. But who were the murderers? What were their motives? And why were no traces of blood, let alone bodies, found?

This puzzling case became known as the Bermagui mystery. No one knows what really happened to Lamont Young and the other four men. Like the people on board the *Mary Celeste*, they apparently vanished into thin air – or disappeared into the deep blue sea.

WRECKED!

9 The ancient wreck

Shifting sands

Imagine that you are staying at the little Killarney Hotel, not far from Tower Hill, about halfway between Warrnambool and Port Fairy on the Victorian coast. Cross over the highway and follow Gorman's Lane down to the beach. Then walk along the sand to the east for about 3 kilometres. Turn your back on the Southern Ocean and face inland. Somewhere beneath the shifting sands of the dunes above the beach lies the answer to one of the greatest mysteries in Australia's history.

The discovery of an ancient wreck

The first Europeans definitely known to have spent time around Port Fairy were whalers and sealers who came to the area during the 1820s and 1830s. These rough-and-ready men killed whales for whalebone and oil, seals for oil and skins. Their work was hard and dangerous.

Three whalers, named Gibson, Wilson and Smith, went out in a small whaleboat hunting seals one day in 1836. Although conditions were rough, they followed a seal into Lady Bay (near where Warrnambool now stands) and then into the mouth of the Hopkins River. Here disaster struck! Waves overturned their boat, and poor Smith was drowned.

The other two men dragged themselves ashore through the surf, and began trudging back along the beach towards Port Fairy. As they rounded the windswept coastline, they saw something amazing – half-buried in the sand dunes lay the hull of a ship. Its design was unusual and it looked ancient. Where had it come from? And how could it have ended up in that place, well above the high water mark?

> ...one of the greatest mysteries in Australia's history

When they reached Port Fairy, Gibson and Wilson told Captain John Mills and his brother, Charles, about this strange sight.

Other sightings of the wreck

The Mills brothers were intrigued by the story and visited the wreck several times during the next few years. One of them tried to cut a piece of wood from the deck but his knife slipped because the timber was as hard as iron. Local Aboriginal people, belonging to the Yangery people, said that the wreck had been there since before they were born. Some also said that yellow men had come to the area long ago. Captain Mills was convinced that the yellow men must have been connected with the wreck and

WRECKED!
The ancient wreck

that they were probably either Spanish or Portuguese.

We may never know the truth about the ship, but at least 30 people claimed that they saw the wreck during the next few decades. Captain Mason from Port Fairy saw it one day in 1846 while riding his horse along the beach towards Warrnambool. Another observer, Jane Manifold, said, 'It was made of dark red wood like mahogany, but strangely designed and constructed. Instead of the familiar planks along the lengths of its sides it had wooden panels.' A farmer once tied a lost calf to the wreck until someone could return for it. It was possible in those days to reach the wreck from nearby Hummock Road, the main track that was established between Warrnambool and Port Fairy. The last person known to have seen it was

> 'It was made of dark red wood like mahogany...'

a mining surveyor named Mr Donnelly. When he saw it in 1880 only a few pieces of wood were sticking out of the sand.

Why did the ancient wreck, as it was often called, disappear? Locals took some of the timber to use on their farms. A blanket of sand probably buried the rest. When Europeans first settled around this area the dunes were covered with shrubs, which kept the sand in place. But their cattle trampled the bushes, and strong

> **SHIP OF ICE**
> According to an old story, a whaling ship was sailing near Antarctica, in about 1860, when all of a sudden its crew heard terrible crashes and groans. Monstrous chunks from nearby cliffs fell into the sea, a huge gap opened up, and out sailed a ghostly ship. Its sails were tattered and torn, and it was covered in ice. Everyone on board was dead – and frozen solid! The whalers believed that the ship had been trapped in the ice for almost 40 years!

winds constantly reshaped the dunes. Sand drifts completely covered the Hummock Road by 1880 – the year in which the wreck was seen for the last time.

Searches and 'relics'

The wreck became known as the Mahogany Ship. Numerous searches for it have been conducted since 1890. Many have been very well organised. Monash University, for example, held an archaeological dig in the area in 1969. Twenty Melbourne sea scouts searched for the wreck in the summer of 1974–75. Fifty-five holes were drilled down through the sand to sea level during a search in 1975–76. In 1992, the Victorian government offered a reward of $250 000 for anyone finding evidence of a buried ship built before 1836. But all the searches have been unsuccessful.

Many objects have been linked to the Mahogany Ship. A diver working on the Port

WRECKED!
The ancient wreck

Fairy Harbour in the 1870s found a 'Spanish rapier' in the Moyne River – but it turned out to be an English sword dropped by a ship's master in 1843. A man named Mr Gilroy uncovered an iron spike and latch in the wreck area during one of the early organised searches. Some people believe that these last two items, now in a showcase at the Flagstaff Hill Maritime Village at Warrnambool, belong to the wreck. Experts have examined an amphora (a narrow necked container with two handles) found on the beach in 1943 – and think that it was probably made in North Africa in the mid-1800s. Other 'relics' have also turned out to be disappointing.

Shipwreck expert Captain Jack Loney says, 'Do you realise that if you believe all the stories linked with timber from the ship there must have been enough to build two or three such vessels?' The objects supposedly made from the timber included a mahogany chair once owned

KILLARNEY STORIES

When I recently stayed at the Killarney Hotel, friendly local people were keen to tell me stories about the Mahogany Ship. 'It was my great uncle who tied the calf up to the wreck,' said one. 'No, no, it was my grandfather,' claimed another. 'Come with me and I'll show you the bridge made from the very timbers,' offered a third man, as he ordered another drink from the bar!

> **THE GEELONG KEYS**
> A workman was digging a lime kiln at Limeburners Point, near Geelong, in September 1847. Almost 5 metres down, in layers of decayed shells and rock, his shovel struck three heavily encrusted old keys. The superintendent of the Port Phillip District (now Victoria), Charles La Trobe, visited the site the next day, saw two keys, and was very interested in them. Somehow the third key had disappeared overnight! The other two keys later also got lost! Could a sailor from a Portuguese caravel have dropped these keys on the beach in the 1500s? If not, how do you think that they could have got into such an odd spot?

by a local family. It had the following words inscribed underneath it: 'Made from Mahogany Ship, wrecked near Tower Hill, July 3rd, 1835. Made by Michael Bradshaw 18–2– .' Sadly, the chair, like the wreck, seems to have disappeared.

A Portuguese caravel?

What kind of vessel was the ancient wreck? Some people say it was really just an old flat-bottomed whaling punt that looked red because its timbers had been stained by whale blood! Others think that it could have been a very old Dutch, Portuguese or Spanish ship.

Historian Kenneth McIntyre has studied ancient maps which he believes show that

WRECKED!
The ancient wreck

Portuguese explorers visited the Victorian coast in 1522 – long before other Europeans came to Australia. He thinks that three Portuguese caravels, commanded by Cristovao de Mendonca, sailed down the east coast of Australia, mapping it, and entered Port Phillip Bay. (Perhaps they landed near present-day Geelong, where one of the sailors dropped some keys, which became known as the Geelong Keys.) Then, according to McIntyre's theory, they

A Portuguese caravel

went on to the Warrnambool area, where one of the caravels was wrecked and the other two turned back. Their discovery of the coastline was kept a secret because they had entered forbidden territory! These waters were reserved for Spanish explorers because of a treaty signed in 1494 by Spain and Portugal.

> ...they had entered forbidden territory!

Glossary

archaeologist	a person who studies civilisations by excavating and examining their remains
ballast	heavy material, such as sand, placed in a ship to make it stable
caravel	a ship of Spanish or Portuguese design (1400s–1600s)
fathom	a unit to measure the depth of water (6 feet – about 1.8 metres)
galleon	a large Spanish sailing-ship
hull	the body of a ship
ketch	a two-masted sailing-boat
lifeline	a rope used in a rescue
mutiny	an open rebellion against people in authority
pinnace	a ship's small boat
salvage	save from a wreck
sinker	a weight used to sink a fishing-line
spar	a pole used for a ship's mast or across a mast to hang sails from
whaler	a person or ship involved in hunting whales
wrecker	a person who deliberately causes a shipwreck, usually by using false lights, in order to plunder the ship

Further reading

1 **The story of the *Speke***
   Phillip Island: In Picture and Story by Joshua Wickett Gliddon (comp.) (Cowes Bush Nursing Hospital, Phillip Island, 1958)
2 **Batavia's Graveyard**
   Islands of Angry Ghosts by Hugh Edwards (Hodder and Stoughton, London, 1966)
   The Voyage of the Batavia by François Pelsaert (Hordern House, Sydney, 1994)
3 **The mutiny on the *Bounty***
   The Mutiny on the Bounty by David Anderson and Margarette Lincoln (Macdonald Children's Books, London, 1989)
4 **The adventures of Eliza Fraser**
   Mrs Fraser and the Fatal Shore by Michael Alexander (Sphere Books Limited, London, 1976, first published in Great Britain by Michael Joseph Ltd, 1970)
   117 Days Adrift by Maurice and Maralyn Bailey (Australasian Publishing Company, Sydney, 1974)
5 **Australia's worst shipwreck**
   Poor Souls, They Perished: The Cataraqui – Australia's Worst Shipwreck by Andrew Lemon and Marjorie Morgan (Hargreen Publishing, North Melbourne, 1986)

WRECKED!
Further reading

6 Eva's story
   Wrecks & Reputations: The Loss of the Schomberg and Loch Ard by Don Charlwood (Angus & Robertson Publishers, Australia, 1977)
   The Loch Ard Disaster by Jack Loney (10th edition, Marine History Publications, c. 1993)

7 'Grace Darling of the West'
   Grace Had an English Heart by Jessica Mitford (Viking, London, 1988) This book is about the original Grace Darling.
   First Lady: A History-Making Solo Voyage Around the World by Kay Cottee (Macmillan, Australia, 1989)

8 The Bermagui mystery
   Five Men Vanished: The Bermagui Mystery by Cyril Pearl (Hutchinson of Australia, Richmond, Victoria, 1978)
   'The *Mary Celeste*' by Richard Garrett, in *Great Unsolved Mysteries* edited by John Canning (Orion, London, 1993, first published 1984)
   The Bermuda Triangle by Charles Berlitz (Panther, England, 1975)

9 The ancient wreck
   The Mahogany Ship by Jack Loney (6th edition, Neptune Press, Geelong, 1985)

Index

Adams, John 35
ancient wreck 84–89

Bailey, Maralyn
  and Maurice 41
Batavia 18–25
Batavia's Graveyard
  22, 23, 24, 25
Baxter, John
  40, 41, 43, 44
Bermagui mystery 74–83
Bermuda Triangle 83
Berry, John 74, 76
Bligh, William 26–30
Bounty 26–8, 32, 34, 35
Bussell, Grace 69–73

Carmichael, Eva
  59, 61–7
Carmichael, Mrs
  59, 61, 65, 68
Carmichael, Raby
  59, 61, 65, 68
Casey, Daniel 76–7
Cataraqui 47–54, 58
Christian, Fletcher
  26–8, 31, 34–5, 36
Cornelisz, Jerome
  19, 20, 22, 23
Cottee, Kay 73

Darge, 'Big Bob'
  41, 42, 43
Darling, Grace 72
de Bye, Jan Pillegran 24
de Vries, Andries
  18, 19, 22–3, 25

Edie 11–12, 17
Edwards, Edward 32–3
Edwards, Hugh 18, 24–5

Finlay, William 48–50
First Lady 73
Ford, George 64–5
Forfarshire 72
Fraser, Eliza 37, 39–46
Fraser, James 37, 39–42

Geelong Keys 89, 90
Georgette 69–70
Gibb, George 59–61
Girona 62
Graham, John 43–4

Hays, Webbye 23, 24
Henderson, Frank 13–15
Hodge, 'Middle Bob'
  44, 45
Howie, David 52–4

Isaacs, Sam 69–73

WRECKED!
Index

Jacobsz, Adriaen 19, 21
Johnson, Dave 24
Johnston, William 74
Jones, Reg 62, 65

Keightley, Henry
 74–6, 79
Killarney Hotel 84, 88
King Island 48–55, 58

lighthouses
 14, 54–8, 59, 72
Lloyd, William 76–7
Loch Ard 59–66
Loch Ard Peacock 68
Loney, Jack 88
Loos, Wouter 23, 24

McIntyre, Kenneth 89–90
Mahogany Ship 87–9
Mary Celeste 82, 83
Mills, John 85–6
Mitchell, Arthur
 61–2, 65

Norfolk Island 35–6

Otter, Charles 43, 44

Pandora 31–3
Pandora (from Greek
 mythology) 30
Pearce, Tom 63–7
Pelsaert, François 19–24
Pereira, Fernando 16
Pharos of Alexandria 57
Phillip Island 11–17
Pitcairn Island 34–6

Rainbow Warrior 16

Speke 12–17
Schneider, Max 76–81
Sténuit, Robert 62
Stirling Castle 37, 39

'The Pines' 11, 12, 15
Till, William 64–5
Tilston, Captain 12, 15
Towers, Thomas 76–7
treasure
 18, 22, 62, 66, 68

van der Mylen, Lucretia
 19, 23, 24

wreckers 12, 14

Youlden, Hendy
 41, 42, 43
Young, Lamont 74–83